H(TO GOD'S UNCHANGING HANDS

Bless and Keep you always Thank You! Towhanna

A STORY OF FAITH, FORGIVENESS, AND VICTORY

BY TOWHANNA BOSTON

KINGDOM JOURNEY PRESS
A DIVISION OF KINGDOM JOURNEY ENTERPRISES
WOODBRIDGE, VA

ISBN 10: 0-9827001-3-X
ISBN 13: 978-0-9827001-3-6

Printed in the United States of America

Published by Kingdom Journey Press
A Division of Kingdom Journey Enterprises
www.kjpressinc.com

DEDICATION

I dedicate this book in Loving Memory of my two precious angels:

Octavia Michelle Suydan
October 1, 1995 – September 11, 2004
And
Christopher Edward Suydan, Jr.
October 22, 1996 – September 11, 2004

"Remember, there is Light at the end of the tunnel!"

Blessed are they that mourn; for they shall be comforted.

St. Matthews 5:4

Every cloud indeed has a silver lining!

Table of Contents

Acknowledgements

First, I want to thank my Lord and Savior, Jesus Christ, Who is the head of my life. I would not be standing if it were not for the Lord, Who is on my side every minute, hour, and step of the way!!

My mom – You are one of the strongest women I know. I thank you for displaying an excellent example of what it is like to trust in The Lord. You have allowed Jesus to sustain you through the loss of a husband, three brothers, and six grandchildren of which four of them were just infants. I am so grateful to God for allowing me to have you as my inspiration.

My daughters Kesha and Trenise – As a mother, I could not have asked for better love and support than what you have given me during the lifetime of your little sister and brother, and since the time of their passing. I thank God for both of you being there through the initial process of me having to learn to live without the "little ones", and for assisting me through each holiday, birthday, and anniversary of their death. I love you both very much!!!

To my brothers John, Stevie, and David – I could not have asked for better brothers. Your love and support have helped me to continue standing, knowing that I was not doing it alone. Your visits during those first twelve months after Tavi and C.J.'s death meant more to me than I can ever express!!! I love you.

Bishop Johnson – I am so appreciative to have you as my pastor. Your continued support and the high level of care and love that you have for the people of God have helped me along this journey.

Thank you for being there to minister the Word to me as I have had to cope with the loss of Tavi and C.J.

Nell, Angela, and Dorothy – Thank you for being there for me then and now. The trip to Atlanta, GA helped to take my mind off the fact that my life will never be the same without Tavi and C.J., and it helped me to maintain balance as I started the re-adjustment process. Oh how I appreciate the times when we (the Golden Girls) literally shut the mall down by shopping until we dropped - LOL; I love you guys!

Casandra Johnson, Founder and CEO of Kingdom Journey Press Publishing Company – I thank God for allowing our paths to cross for such a time as this. I appreciate you for being the woman of God you are and allowing Him to use you for the up-building of His Kingdom. Your level of love, compassion, and professionalism is as a very rare diamond or gem in today's society. My experience with you and the Kingdom Journey Press family has been one I will never forget, and if I could do it all over again, I choose you!!! Thank you for encouraging and inspiring me to keep pushing during the process of this project. Love you much as a publisher, sister, and friend!

To the Tribe of Asher and the entire Greater Morning Star Family…..Thank you from the bottom of my heart!

Thanks to everyone for your prayers, phone calls, encouragement, and love.

Introduction

*H*old *To God's Unchanging Hands* is an inspirational book about holding on to the promises of God, even as we journey through the storms of life. As a result of what God has done in my life, I hope to encourage everyone who will read my story of God's goodness, which has allowed me to triumph even in the midst of tragedy.

After the death of my two youngest children, I was inspired to write a book to encourage others who have lost loved ones and are in need of support during the grief process.

As my daughter Octavia, affectionately known as Tavi, and my son Christopher Jr., affectionately known as C.J., were crossing the street with their dad, they were struck down by a suspect who was fleeing police during a high speed chase. The tragic accident happened in a residential neighborhood in Washington, DC on September 11, 2004. Both of my children were to celebrate their birthdays the following month; Tavi's birthday was October 1st and C.J.'s was October 22nd. Their ages at the time of death were eight and seven years old, with Tavi being the oldest.

Perhaps you can imagine the pain my heart was feeling.

When Tavi and C.J. were taken at such young ages, I initially felt like God was punishing me for having seven pregnancies, but only giving birth to four children. I am grateful however that I have come to know that He is a forgiving God.

I truly thank God for loaning my children to me and allowing me to have the opportunity to instruct, guide, and love them. My desire however was to raise them to become the adults He designed for them to be, with hopes that they would avoid making the same mistakes I made.

I never imagined that I would not raise all four of my children until they reached the age of adulthood. The reality is that as parents, we never expect for our children to precede us in death.

I have two older girls, Kesha and Trenise, who are six years apart. My son C.J. was the baby, and there were 11 months between him and my youngest daughter Tavi. With all of the hard work that comes with parenting, I can truly say I really enjoyed being a mom to all four of my children.

As I was initially going through the process of learning to live with the loss of my two youngest children, God allowed me to experience true joy, peace, comfort, and healing, and I thank Him for that. I know it may sound strange to some that I was able to give God thanks and praise for my tragedy, but it was through praise that God truly strengthened and healed my heart. I am so, so convinced that God does not make mistakes. Although we do not always understand, God knows what He is doing and He does all things well!!!

Matthew 5:4 reads, *Blessed are they that mourn: for they shall be comforted.* In my own personal experience of losing Tavi and C.J., God removed the sting of my pain four months after calling them to be with Him; and what I have learned through this experience is there is no one who can comfort you like Christ.

Now I invite you to sit back and allow me to share the first year of my journey after the loss of my babies.

.

Chapter 1

9/11 - The Day My World Was Forever Changed

On that fateful day of September 11, 2004, my life was forever changed. When I lost my two youngest children, I thought about all the families that lost loved ones three years prior on September 11, 2001. It completely blew my mind to say the least.

September 11th is really not a good day for many in the natural, but in the spiritual, it's about the Lord moving people forward in what they were really born to do.

Most of the world is familiar with what took place on September 11, 2001 when terrorists associated with the Al Qaeda group used airplanes to launch attacks on the twin towers in New York; then they used another plane to hit the Pentagon in Arlington, VA, and they also took over a fourth plane that they were trying to divert to Washington, DC to strike other buildings, but the passengers forced it down in a field in Somerset, PA.

The entire day turned into a total day of devastation..........what in the world was going on here?

I believe God was trying to get so many people's attention.

God could have stopped the terrorist attacks just as He could have not allowed the suspect to run that red light, killing Tavi and C.J.

After the attacks, many churches were packed out with people crying out for help to cope with what happened on the tragic day of Tuesday, September 11, 2001. Many people did not know what to do or how to move forward without their mom, dad, child, wife, husband, sister, brother, and friends. The pain was unbearable to say the least, but God allowed each one of the family members who were left to get through it because they are still here 10 years later.

Some people allowed the Lord to help them forgive the terrorists and honor the life of their loved ones in a positive manner, while fulfilling whatever their purpose is in Christ. Others remained angry, and may be still angry today, and have allowed the pain to intensify.

On September 11, 2004, exactly three years to the day of the terrorist attacks, I was in so much shock, and thought about how the families who were impacted by the terrorist attacks must have felt.

On every anniversary of the September 11th terrorist attacks, I think of the families who lost loved ones on that fateful day. I immediately begin praying for them because I know that the Lord already has people who are praying for me and my family.

As I was writing this book, I began wondering if or how many of the family members who lost loved ones on that tragic day were serving the Lord, or whether they had found their purpose in life.

I cannot believe that it has been seven years since the death of my kids, but I do not want my turn to come and I have not fulfilled the things that God has purposed for me to do.

If you do not know what you are supposed to be doing in life, I challenge you today to seek God, ask Him to give you clarity in the direction He wants you to go, and allow Him to use your loss, your pain, and your trial to do a greater work for Him in Jesus Name!!

Towhanna Boston

Chapter 2

The Rainbow After The Storm

Rainbows are typically known to have about seven different colors. Often, it begins with the color red, which signifies hard, disruptive, difficult, and downright uncomfortable; and ends with violet, which is calm, soft, peaceful, and signifies the end of the storm.

People may have different beliefs about the meanings of the rainbow and its colors. Therefore I would like for you to compare what you believe the rainbow means in relation to trials that you may be currently experiencing, or have faced at some point in your life.

Whenever I think about a rainbow, my mind goes back to Noah during the time of the flood and how God made a covenant between man and Himself that He would never again destroy the earth by water.

Perhaps the color red from the rainbow as discussed in the Bible in Genesis signifies the beginning of the flood, or the tunnel of destruction in a person's life; and the violet color in the rainbow comes at the end of the storm, which is bright and full of life. This is where I am reminded of the Scripture in Psalms 30:5 which says, *Weeping may endure for a night, but joy cometh in the morning.*

This passage of Scripture again is a reminder of a promise made and kept by our God.

As you continue reading, perhaps you will see how the rainbow fits my experience during the loss of Tavi and C.J. For me, violet represents passion and life; oh how I treasure the many fond memories of Tavi and C.J.'s life and remember the things that made them happy. On the other end, red signifies how losing them the way I did and when I did has been uncomfortable, difficult, and hard, thus causing deep hurt and pain. It's a day I will never forget!!

The colors in the middle of the rainbow represent the stages I experienced between violet and red. Orange and yellow causes me to remember their smiles and the sun that shined so bright through them; the heart they had for others, always sharing, caring, and helping. Blue, as in the sky, represents the air they now breathe, and allows me to picture them being God's little helpers. Violet just doesn't signify royalty as most people know it to mean, but it also represents peace, or light, after experiencing a really dark time.

The rainbow is a reminder that we must endure the storms and rain, with the clouds, in order to obtain that silver lining. Storms are often rough, hard, and destructive, but when they come to an end, the sun and the rainbow are there shining bright.

Nobody but God can take tragedy and turn it into something as good and beautiful as a rainbow, which helps to make life worth living. ☺

Chapter 3

Our Favorite Things

Tavi's Favorite Things

Oh, how I liked my favorite things
"Lifting His Name on High",
Is what I liked to sing.

Each day I played,
Dolls were the best.
Barbie and the Bratz,
Could there be anything else.

Now don't forget
My love for food.
Not only did I like to eat,
But desired to be a great chef, too.
Watching the Food Network
Was such a delight.
For you see learning in all capacities
Was one of the great loves of my life.

And now I have graduated,
To my mansion in the sky.
Spending all day with Jesus,
In my new home on high.

C.J.'s Favorite Things

Oh, how I liked my favorite things,
"Get Your Mind on Jesus",
Is what I liked to sing.

Each day I played,
Super heroes were the best.
Buzz Lightyear, Spiderman and Batman,
Could there be anything else.

Now don't forget,
My love for the game.
Hunting cicadas, football and karate,
Would be my road to fame.

I worked real hard,
And a yellow belt I obtained.
Now my work is finished and I'm happy to say,
That the ultimate goal, a crown of righteousness,
I have gained.

Chapter 4

The Day Tavi and C.J. Were Killed

On September 11, 2004, I arose early in the morning to prepare Tavi and C.J. to attend their dad's company picnic. At the time, I was not aware that this was going to be a day that my life would be forever changed.

We often referred to Tavi and C.J. as "the little ones".

After I laid out the "little ones'" clothes, I told them to take their showers. As everyone was getting dressed, we started talking about last year's picnic. C.J. remembered how big the shrimp were and said he was going to eat more this time.

I asked C.J. to bring me some back, and then Tavi said, "What else do you want on your plate mommy?"

I said, "Whatever they may have – barbeque chicken, potato salad, and anything else you think mommy will like."

We laughed, and then we finished getting dressed.

As I reflect back on this conversation, I encourage parents to cherish each and every moment you have with your kids and family because you never know when it may be your last time together.   After losing Tavi and C.J., I came to realize that spending quality time with children is so very important, from the time they are born until the time they are on their own!

I remember the "little ones" being so excited about spending the day with their dad. I would always anoint and pray for God to keep and protect them, however on this particular day, I did not. You can probably imagine how I felt after their deaths, where I was initially blaming myself because I did not pray for them that day.

Another thing I always did was give them a kiss and hug before leaving the house. Again, I did not hug and kiss them on this day.

We often take so much for granted, however we never know when it will be our last time seeing our loved ones, therefore it's important to cherish every moment. For those who give hugs and kisses to your loved ones, continue to do so. For those who do not – you may want to start!

Since the kids were going to be out with their dad for most of the day, I made plans to go to the credit union and take care of other business. I did not have a car at the time, therefore I had to use public transportation. Because it was a Saturday and the credit union closed early, I had to leave before their dad came to pick them up. When I left to catch the bus, I told the kids I may not be back before their dad arrived, but that I would see them later; I did not know however that I would never see them again.

Life is very short, therefore I just cannot stress it enough that you must cherish every moment you have with your children. While we know <u>when</u> we were born and even <u>how</u> we were born, we do not know when or how we are going to leave this earth. For this reason, I will pause right here and ask you to take a break, right this minute, and ask yourself these questions:

1) If I were to die right now – this very minute, am I ready?
2) What is the condition of my heart?

What are your answers?

These are just some questions for you to think about because we have to be ready when our time comes!!

As I headed out to catch the bus, I looked at my watch and saw that I had some extra time before my bus was scheduled to arrive. I decided to walk to Burger King for breakfast, which I got and ate at the bus stop.

As I was waiting, I heard a voice say, "Praise the Lord!"

I looked up and saw that it was one of the brothers from my church. He offered me a ride to the subway station and since the bus had not come yet, I accepted his offer. He dropped me off at the nearest subway station, I thanked him, and then he drove off.

As I arrived inside the station, there was a train waiting, so I got on and took a sit near the window. As I was sitting there, I started thinking of everything I needed to do before the kids returned home. As the train began to move, I noticed there were a lot of people who were up and out early for it to be Saturday – perhaps they were all on their way to work.

The train ride was smooth, but it took a long time to get to Springfield, VA.

After I got off the train, there was a bus waiting, so I started walking fast to avoid missing it.

I got on the bus and asked the driver if he was going to Springfield Mall.

He said "yes", so I sat down and after a few more people boarded, the bus pulled off. After getting off the bus at Springfield Mall, I still had to walk about four blocks to get to the credit union. I got there fast and was just amazed that it took very little time to walk those four blocks. As I walked through the doors of the credit union, I noticed the line was kind of short, so I knew it would not take hardly any time to get in and out.

After I finished at the credit union, I walked back to the mall to catch the bus back to the subway station. When I arrived at the mall, there were not any buses anywhere in site because on Saturdays, the buses run less frequent than during the work week. I saw a cab though and asked the driver how much the fare would be to go from the mall to the subway station.

The driver replied, "Oh, about $4.00".

I said "great", so then I got in the cab and the driver took off.

After arriving at the subway station, again there was a train waiting to leave. I was sort of tickled because everything seemed to be moving along so well. As I think back – things were moving because the Lord already knew what was taking place as I was headed back.

Writing this bring tears to my eyes because although I did not know it, my children's lives were being taken at the same time and

I was not there. The question I had to ask though is whether I could have handled seeing them being killed. Maybe not, this perhaps is why God allowed things to be as they were.

While riding the train home, once again I began to think of all the things that had to be done once the kids returned home – such as groceries, laundry, and Tavi's hair. I was also hoping to have enough time to get C.J.'s haircut, but I was not sure whether they would arrive before the barbershop closed.

Anyway, once the train arrived at my stop, I noticed that I had just missed the bus, and it would be about an hour before another bus was to come. While I was waiting for the next bus, I initially decided that I would go to the beauty supply store to pick up a relaxer for Tavi's hair and a few other items. Instead, I stopped by the pay phone at the subway station first to call and check on Trenise and to see whether the "little ones" had been picked up yet.

When Trenise answered the phone, I asked if Tavi and C.J. had been picked up. She said "yes", so I asked what time they left. She said about 10:30, but then went on to tell me that their dad had just called and asked if I was home yet. She had told him no and then she stated that he told her not to leave the house and to have me call him as soon as I returned! She said, "Mom I think you better call him now because he sounded like he was crying."

I said "okay – let me call him now before I go to the beauty supply store and I will call you back!"

I hung up the phone with Trenise and then called Chris on his Sprint cellphone. Someone picked up, but it wasn't him – it was one of his co-workers.

I said "I am trying to reach Chris."

His co-worker told me that I may want to call him on his Nextel cellphone. I hung up and dialed Chris' Nextel cell phone, and he picked up asking where I was. I told him that I was at the subway station waiting for the next bus because I had just missed one.

He told me to stay there and he was going to have one of his co-workers pick me up.

I asked, "Where exactly will your co-worker be taking me?"

Chris said, "He will bring you to the hospital."

I asked, "Why is he taking me there?"

Chris said, "I will tell you when you get here."

I then asked, "What kind of car should I look out for?"

He described the truck and then we hung up the phone.

After hanging up the telephone with Chris, I called Trenise back and told her that he was sending someone to pick me up and take me to the hospital.

She asked, "Why are you going to the hospital? What happened?"

I told her I did not know because he did not tell me. Then I told her to put her clothes on because I may have to send someone to pick her up.

She said "okay", and we hung up the phone.

When Chris' co-worker arrived, we greeted each other as I got into the truck. We briefly exchanged small talk by comparing the difference between living in Maryland and Virginia. After that, the ride to the hospital was very quiet with some music playing very low. I was thinking that the kids were hurt, but never imagined they were dead.

Chris' co-worker knew what happened, but I guess he felt it was not his place to tell me. You can never be prepared for losing close loved ones, regardless of whether it's expected or unexpected!

I want to take time to thank God for knowing what is best and allowing us to cast our cares on Him, meaning our losses, our trials, our questions, our concerns, our ideas, as well as our uncertainties. God knows what to do, how to do it, and when to do it; and we can depend on Him for all things.

As you continue reading, remember there is nothing too hard for God and He will bring you through your trials. You may not be able to see it or know how you are going to make it when you are going through it, but nothing catches God by surprise. Hebrews 13:8 says *Jesus Christ the same yesterday, and today, and forever.*

Towhanna Boston

Chapter 5

Arriving at the Hospital

As we arrived at the hospital and pulled into the emergency room entrance, Chris' co-worker phoned him to let him know we had arrived. Chris came out of the emergency room entrance door to meet us.

Chris and I spoke after I got out of the truck. Then I followed as he walked through the emergency room toward the back where I thought Tavi and C.J. were being examined by the doctor. I remember seeing several police officers standing next to the room where Chris took me.

Once I entered the room, I began to get nervous because I did not see my babies. Instead, I remember seeing a table and some chairs lined up along the wall. I also remember someone asking Chris if they should go ahead and bring the doctor in. That's when I began to ask Chris what was going on.

Chris told me to sit down, so I sat down and asked again, "What is going on?"

He said "Tavi and C.J. were in an accident – they were hit by a car."

Then I said, "Okay, so what did the doctor say?"

That's when he said, "They are no longer with us!"

I looked at him and said, "What do you mean they are no longer with us?"

He said, "They died."

My body went straight into shock and I screamed so loud and cried so hard that I thought I was going to have a heart attack. My blood pressure went up. I remember screaming and shouting, "I want to see my kids; I want to see my kids!"

The social worker who was there said they would let me see Tavi and C.J. as soon as I calmed down. She said I needed to be prepared for what I was about to see, therefore they really needed me to calm down enough to listen to them. Then she said, "I know this is the worst news that you could ever have received, and I am so, so sorry for what happened to your children. We are going to bring the doctor in to speak with you and then I will take you to where your children are, and you can sit with them for as long as you want."

While waiting for the doctor to come in, and as I was still crying, I began to give God thanks for knowing what is best, and then I asked Him to help me!!

As the doctor came into the room and sat down, he said, "I want you to know we had a great team working on your children and we did our very best to try and revive them."

As I sat crying so hard and waiting for them to take me to see Tavi and C.J., a million things went running through my mind. I started thinking about how I would ever get through life not having them anymore. Then God allowed a sudden peace to come over me long enough to hear what the social worker was explaining in reference to the "little ones" appearance. She shared that they both had suffered abrasions to their faces, C.J. still had blood running from his ear due to the head trauma he suffered, and they both were still hooked up with tubes. I just sat there listening in shock; not believing what I was hearing.

After the social worker finished explaining the kids' condition, their father told me he had already called my pastor, Bishop Johnson, and that his mom and dad also already knew.

Initially I was very shocked when he said he called Bishop Johnson, but I knew that it was nobody but God Who touched his heart to make that call because Chris had stopped coming to the church we used to attend together a long time ago.

By this time I had asked a friend from church to pick up my daughter Trenise and bring her to the hospital; then I called Kesha and asked whether there was someone who could give her a ride to the hospital. I told her it was because of Tavi and C.J. She responded that she could get a ride, and I told her to come as soon as she could. The rest of my family lived in Philadelphia so they found out what happened later that evening after I got home.

The social worker asked if I was okay and whether I was ready to go and sit with Tavi and C.J., and I told her "yes".

At that moment, we left the room to go where Tavi and C.J.'s lifeless bodies were. As I walked in, the tears began to flow again, very, very heavy and my chest felt like someone had walked on it!! I walked over to Tavi first and rubbed her hair and her hands and just cried. Her lips had already turned blue, but she looked as though she was just sleeping. Then I walked over to C.J. and rubbed his hair and his hand, crying "my baby, my baby – oh God please help me!!"

I looked up with my eyes closed, talking to the Lord in my mind saying, "Lord you didn't just take one, but you took both of my babies. Please help me Lord, and I still give you the glory and praise because You and only You know what is best."

At that time, the Lord reminded me of the book of Job and how he lost his seven sons and three daughters in the same day and at the same time. It was not just the fact that Job lost all of his children, but the fact that satan had to obtain permission from God to do what he did, which God allowed because He knew that Job was not going to give up on Him!

You have to read the book of Job in the Bible to understand what I am explaining. Job continued to worship God even in the midst of his loss. He held on to God's unchanging hand and did not let go.

When I thought about Job, it was so very encouraging to me!! So I dried my tears and proceeded out of the room. As I was walking, I looked up and saw the assistant pastor of my church, Elder Davis, coming down the hall. I walked up to him and cried in his arms; then I showed him the room where Tavi and C.J. were.

As Chris and I stood by Tavi and C.J., with tears flowing down our faces, Elder Davis began to pray for God to give us strength and grace through this tragic time of our lives. After he finished praying, we all walked out from the room where the little ones' lifeless bodies laid and went back into the room where I first received the bad news of their death. By this time, some of the other members from my church had arrived as well as Bishop Johnson and Chris' parents.

While we sat waiting for Trenise and Kesha to arrive, Chris took Bishop Johnson to the room where Tavi and C.J. were. I sat in the chair trying to figure out how we were going to pay for the funeral. The reason why I was so concerned about the cost of the funeral was because I remembered that during the time I was laid off from work, I did not have any kind of insurance - health, auto, or life! At the time of their death, I had only been with my new full-time job for six months, and I could not remember if I had signed the kids up for life insurance.

While my mind was racing, Trenise arrived. We sat her down and Chris explained what happened to Tavi and C.J. She screamed and cried uncontrollably and began saying "I want to see them, please let me see them!" Chris and I didn't think that was a good idea, in fact we didn't let anyone except Bishop Johnson and Elder Davis see Tavi and C.J. We knew that Trenise would not have been able to handle the sight of them.

Chris' mom and dad sat with Trenise to try calming her down. I went into the next room to have my blood pressure checked by the nurse. I have diabetes, which caused me to also have high blood pressure, and when my body went into shock, my pressure level increased.

After I had my blood pressure checked, I asked Bishop Johnson if he would preach Tavi and C.J.'s eulogy during their home going service. I told him and Elder Davis that I didn't even know where to begin with putting everything together because I had never lost anyone this close. They both agreed that they would take care of it. They said for me to just tell them what I wanted, but I did not have to think about it for right now.

I truly thank God for Bishop Johnson and Elder Davis because they are always there when any of the members from our church have extreme challenges; and let me tell you, our church has had so many members who have gone home to be with the Lord!!

Once again, ask yourself, "If I were to die at this very moment, would I be ready? Have I fulfilled God's plan and purpose for my life?" Think about it, and if the answer is "no", then do something about it!!!

As we sat, still waiting for Kesha to arrive, Bishop Johnson and Elder Davis continued to pray. Chris' dad began to cry out loud, and as he and mom were comforting Trenise, dad pulled out a picture of the "little ones", which caused him to weep even more. Then Bishop Johnson stood and asked that we all stay for prayer, and he continued to pray for the situation. Once prayer was over, I stepped out into the hall and noticed Kesha standing at the information desk, so I called out to her. She looked up and began to walk towards me, so I guided her into the room where everyone was waiting.

I sat Kesha down and then Chris came back into the room so he could explain to her that Tavi and C.J. were in an accident and they had died. I felt so sorry for Kesha because she lives on her own and we did not see her that much. In fact, the last time she had seen Tavi and C.J. was June, and they died in September.

When Kesha learned the news, she screamed and cried so hard until she was choking. I tried to comfort her, but as I hugged her I began to break down and cry again. I was so emotionally drained that I was ready to go home, so my friend gave Trenise and me a ride home.

This was truly a day I will never forget, and even now, I can still remember it as if it were yesterday.

Towhanna Boston

Chapter 6

Informing Family and Friends

Once I arrived home, I started making phone calls to family members in Philadelphia. First I informed my mom, while crying at the same time. I explained to her that Tavi and C.J. were crossing the street with their dad and were hit by a suspect who had been involved in a high speed police chase. I told her the suspect hit them so hard that they were killed instantly, however they were not pronounced dead until they reached the hospital.

My mom said, "Oh Towhanna, we are on our way."

I didn't have to call anybody else in Philly because my mom started making calls for me.

Then I called a friend from work, along with my supervisor and manager, to let them know I would not be at work the following week because of the death of my children. After being home for about an hour, people from my church, friends who were in the military with me, and co-workers began to come to my house; you know news, good or bad, travels fast!

I once read that God's voice is heard in the storms of life. Well truly the thought of losing Tavi and C.J. was not just a storm, but to me it was an unexplained hurt and I didn't know how I was going to continue my life without them. I knew my life would never be the same; but God's peace and grace have carried me in such a way that those who don't understand would have thought I was glad that my children were gone. Isaiah 26:3 tells us that *Thou [meaning God] wilt keep him, [you, everybody] in perfect peace whose mind is stayed on Thee: because he trusteth in thee*!!

Now let me express the greatness of God's peace. Up until 12:00 midnight, there were many people coming and going from my house. There were moments when I cried, and then moments when I remembered something Tavi or C.J. said or did, and it made me laugh. I thank God for His word in Psalm 29:11 which says, *The Lord will give strength unto his people; the Lord will bless his people with peace.* Glory!! Thank you Jesus that there is no peace like the peace of God!

Although I had support from my church, family, friends and co-workers, nobody could ease my mind and my aching heart but God! You have to trust that God knows what He is doing with your life.

I ended up going to sleep really late due to the many phone calls and visits. I was truly glad and thankful for the visits because people were there to assist with and comfort my middle daughter who was so devastated that she got sick and threw up all the food she had eaten prior to coming to the hospital. I began asking the Lord to help her because I didn't have the energy to carry both of our grief. In fact, both of my older girls got sick and could not eat or sleep. My oldest daughter, as I mentioned before, lives on her own so I felt bad for her that night. I really wished she had come home with me from the hospital, but she went home instead.

The next day, September 12, 2004, was a Sunday, and I had an early start. No sooner than when I had taken my shower and gotten dressed, the phone began ringing. At that moment, I was trying to get prepared for what I knew would be a really busy day.

The phone call was from my mom telling me that she and my brothers were on their way from Philadelphia and should arrive to my home within a few hours. While waiting on them to arrive, two of my friends from church came and sat with me for several hours until others from the church arrived. The service at my church is usually over by 1:45 PM, therefore my apartment started to become really full at around 2:30 PM.

A friend from high school also came to visit from Virginia Beach, along with some people from my neighborhood who heard what happened on the news. By the time my mom arrived, I was so tired and drained that I just wanted to lie down.

I was so tired from not being able to sleep and then having to get up every hour. Each time I got up, I just got down on my knees and prayed for God to help me through this. So I continued greeting everyone, then one of my cousins was there serving people food and drinks.

When the missionaries from my church arrived, they had a lot of food, so people were able to eat and introduce themselves to each other. I finally made it over to the kitchen where my youngest brother was standing. He and I just embraced each other and began to cry so hard and for so long.

My brother and his wife had just lost twin boys. She miss-carried just a few months prior to Tavi and C.J.'s death, therefore my brother was still experiencing a lot of grief.

During all of this, I still accepted some phone calls and had people taking messages from others. My boss called and her boss called to offer their deepest sympathy. Then there were so many flowers sent until my apartment started looking like it could have been a floral shop.

I was glad to know that so many people cared and gave the emotional support we needed. Even with all the excellent and wonderful support, none of it could totally ease my pain or take away the thoughts I was having of never seeing my babies again!

As time came for some of the missionaries and others to leave, we gathered for prayer. One of the leaders from the church and his wife were there to lead the prayer. As he prayed for God to give us strength and grace through this tragedy, we began thanking God for His mercy, for knowing all things, and for the strength that He had already given us.

Many of the visitors left once the prayer was over, including my friend that had driven from Virginia Beach. We hugged each other and she said she would call once she made it home. My brothers also got on the road to drive back to Philly, but my mom stayed with me for the entire week to assist with planning Tavi and C.J.'s home-going service.

I am thankful to everyone who was able to help with my girls. My oldest daughter's boss brought her to my apartment, and she stayed the entire week too. I was glad, and I thanked Kesha's boss for looking out for her.

I am also grateful to the president of our church usher board because she was able to get my daughters to eat. The assistant pastor along with some other leaders from the church also prayed with my girls who continued to cry so hard because they were having such a difficult time handling the death of their little brother and sister. I am so grateful to God for providing the support we needed.

Throughout this story you will hear praying, praising, and pressing because I am convinced that you cannot get through life's trials without the help of God. If you are looking for a sad story here, let me tell you there isn't one. I don't have a sad story!

Yes, what happened to Tavi and C.J. was sad, heart breaking, and painful, but I continued to pray, continued to praise, and continued to press my way through this difficult time in my life.

Prayer will get you back on the right track.

You may ask, "What do you mean prayer will get you on the right track?"

Well, when trials are hard, especially as a result of losing children or any close loved ones, prayer is the communication to God where others can't understand how and what you feel. Prayer will help you to become focused and prevent the "why me" questions. Prayer will keep you from hurting all those who you believe were involved with the cause of your loved one's death.

Elder Davis often says praise strengthens the heart of the bereaved. In the midst of your trials, continue to thank God and give Him praise for knowing what is best for you and your family. Then you will begin to see the strength He will give you, which will blow your mind.

With that amazing strength from God, it allows you to press. Pressing will prevent you from giving up on life; pressing will also prevent you from giving up on yourself, and it will prevent you from giving up on God. Pressing will cause you to remain determined to survive in spite of the terrible thing that has taken place.

So as you go through the storms of life, remember the three P's (Pray, Praise, and Press). Don't give up!!! HOLD TO GOD'S UNCHANGING HANDS!!!!!!! WHEW.......I FEEL A SHOUT COMING!

Chapter 7

Just Yesterday

Just yesterday, I heard your laugh, saw your face and watched your smile

Just yesterday, I held you close, and we talked for a little while
You told me how your day went, and I told you of mine
Then, later I called you in from playing, it was dinnertime

Just yesterday I said your prayers with you, and kissed you before you hopped in the sack,

Just yesterday, you called me at work and said, "If you can catch this message, call right back,"

Just yesterday, after your homework, we sat and watched cartoons
And, although I never admitted it, I enjoyed watching them too
I remembered times when you got sick, and nursing you back to health. I remembered all the pride I felt, 'cause you knew Jesus for yourself

But today, it seems you've left me, and although it's hard to deal
My comfort comes in knowing, it was in my Father's will
My tears will still be falling; my heart still has to mend

Towhanna Boston

Yet, my joy comes in the morning, for I will see you again

Just yesterday you were in my arms
But today, you are in the loving arms of our Savior
I look forward to the tomorrow when we will be united again

Until then,
Your Loving Mother

Chapter 8

October

I remember October being an extremely hard month. By this time, the phone calls and visits had slowed down, or even come to a halt. I often felt alone, even though I knew I was not really alone.

By this time, I had cleaned out Tavi and C.J.'s closets and given their toys away to their friends. I would sometimes go into their room and cry, not believing they were gone and never coming back again.

Their home-going service was videotaped, so sometimes I would lie in C.J.'s bed and watch it for comfort. You may think it is crazy to watch a videotape of their home going service, but we had a good time praising God during the service. It was like being in service on Sunday, except there were caskets in the front of the church.

Bishop Johnson preached his heart out, as he always does, so watching the service gave me some relief from my tears. Perhaps you have to see it in order to understand what I am saying!

As noted on the dedication page of this book, you can see that Tavi and C.J. both had birthdays in the month of October. Tavi's birthday came first on October 1st. She was eight years old at the time of her death, so she would have been turning nine on her next birthday.

On the morning of Tavi's birthday, Trenise went to school and I got up and prayed and proceeded to get dressed. After getting dressed, I went to the store and bought some beautiful pink flowers to put on Tavi's grave.

Tavi and C.J. were buried together, with C.J. on top. We had separate markers with their pictures on them, with each one having a vase for flowers.

After buying the flowers, I went to the grave site, which is about a seven minute drive from where I lived at the time. I got out of the car and placed the flowers in the vase. Then I started crying so hard, saying over and over and over again, "Mommy really misses you!" Even as I am writing at this very moment, I feel the tears in my eyes. I am not hurting any more, but I know I will always miss them and everything about them.

After I stopped crying, I sat in my car and began praying and talking to God and asking Him how were we going to get through this. I told the Lord that He was the only one Who could get us through this difficult journey after experiencing such a great loss.

Then I left the gravesite and went back home to wait for Trenise to arrive from school so we could pick Kesha up, and then all go back to the gravesite together. Initially we were all supposed to go together, but I felt the need to go alone that morning and take Kesha and Trenise later that same day.

While I was home, I continued to pray and talk to God, asking for help with the unbearable sadness I was feeling. My entire life had changed and I was not prepared for the adjustment that had to take place. My mind went to <u>Hebrews 13:5</u> which lets us know that Jesus will never leave nor forsake us. This is having God's divine presence and Him being with us as we deal with difficult times in life. Again this works with us having faith as we pray, praise and press; being determined to allow God to comfort us while asking for His continued help and holding to His unchanging hand.

I felt a little better by the time Trenise made it home from school, and was now ready to take the girls to Tavi and C.J.'s gravesite. I prayed for God to give them both the strength they needed because I could barely help myself. Our God is so good because He did just that!

Trenise and I went to pick up Kesha, and then we all went over to the gravesite. The sun was shining so bright, and even though it was October, it felt like spring.

We pulled up to the gravesite and got out of the car. I thought the girls were going to break down and start crying and screaming, but they did really well all because of God! They saw the flowers that I had put in the vase and said they were beautiful. Then we walked around looking at other gravesites. We talked, laughed, and just enjoyed one another.

We stayed for about 30 minutes, and our visit was really pleasant. When I got home, I began to give God praise, and I thanked Him for helping Trenise and Kesha emotionally. I also spoke with my mom and my brothers, letting them know that we had a pleasant visit.

My middle and youngest brothers both said they would drive down to visit the gravesite with me for C.J.'s birthday, which was two weeks later. I thought that was so sweet of my brothers! C.J.'s birthday was October 22nd and he would have been eight.

The next few weeks were full of mixed feelings. I had not yet gone back to work but was making plans to return. During that time however, some very good friends of mine paid for me to take a vacation for a week in Atlanta, GA. We call ourselves the GOLDEN GIRLS.

I was really excited and had so much fun with them. We went to see a play called "Friends & Lovers", which deals with relationships, and it was very funny. We also ate at Gladys Knight and Ron Winans Chicken and Waffles. The hotel room was also lovely. We had a chance to go to church and also tour the home where Dr. Martin Luther King, Jr. was born and lived as a child, and the church where he was the Co-Pastor and also preached many of his sermons.

Before coming back to the hotel, we shopped until we dropped. Somehow, shopping makes women feel good - LOL! We actually closed the mall down and security had to put us out.

During the day time, God allowed me to be fine, but while lying in bed at night, I would quietly cry for my children, longing for their smiles, kisses, and hugs.

Once the trip had come to an end, it was time for C.J.'s birthday. My brothers drove down as promised and it was a beautiful visit; once again, look at God!

My youngest brother took Tavi and C.J's death extremely hard. You would have thought they were his children.

While at the gravesite, we all talked and remembered the happy times with Tavi and C.J. while they were alive. After visiting the grave, we went to Ruby Tuesday and had lunch before my brothers got on the road to drive back to Philly and Jersey.

You better know that God does all things well and He does not make mistakes!

Shortly after Tavi and C.J.'s birthday, I went back to work part time to help Trenise get used to the fact that they were not going to be home with her after school. They all got home from school within 3 to 5 minutes of each other, therefore she was used to them being home with her until I got in from work. Now she had to accept the fact that they were never coming back. Let me tell you, this process was extremely hard for her and it began to show in her behavior. She had gotten off the honor roll and just started not caring about anything anymore.

You know I did some serious praying because children handle grief differently from adults. I was not trying to hurt her though because I knew she was also in the midst of dealing with her own grief.

I continued to pray, and then I had a talk with Trenise regarding the way she was responding to Tavi and C.J.'s death in a negative manner. I let her know that the way she was responding was not going to bring them back. I explained to her that I could get a counselor to assist with her grief process, but she said "NO", then she got herself together……..

Lord, I just want to thank you!

Chapter 9

The Very First Holidays

I remember the first Thanksgiving without my babies; I gave God thanks for the many invitations we received to have Thanksgiving dinner with so many wonderful saints and friends, and also my mother-in-law. While we were grateful for each invitation, my girls and I decided to visit my youngest brother in New Jersey for about four days.

It was hard having Thanksgiving without Tavi and C.J., so I had to just take one hour at a time and give God thanks for letting me share another day with family.

As we celebrated our first Thanksgiving without Tavi and C.J., we sat down remembering things they would say and do that made us laugh. One fond memory is when we celebrated my mother's 60th birthday. We videotaped Tavi and my nieces singing happy birthday to my mom. Then while we were eating the wonderful dinner that was prepared by my youngest brother and his wife, C.J. finished his collard greens and asked if he could have some more of those holler greens because that's what he thought they were called. We all laughed so hard, and then we told him the correct way to pronounce them.

My middle brother asked C.J. if the greens were so good that they made him want to holler. We all started laughing again.

The first Thanksgiving was enjoyable, but after we stopped laughing, it got kind of quiet. I went off to be myself and I began to cry because I was wishing that Tavi and C.J. were with us. I also began talking to the Lord in the midst of my tears, knowing that He knew what was best for Tavi and C.J.

I was assured that God will and is able to see us through the rough times in our lives.

QUITTING IS NOT AN OPTION!!!!!

Christmas was different, and much harder. Tavi and C.J. always made our Christmas so special with their excitement, questions, and the joy they expressed when they woke up to see the tree full of wonderful gifts and toys. They knew the true reason for celebrating Christmas though, which is the birth of Jesus.

After we had prayer to thank God for allowing us to see another Christmas, Tavi and C.J. would be ready to open their gifts.

Well Christmas of 2004 was not the same. We were missing Tavi and C.J.'s voices telling Trenise to get up, and them not wanting breakfast because they were so excited and ready to open their presents.

After I woke up, I fell on my knees and cried as I prayed asking God to help me.

My middle brother drove down from Philly on Christmas Eve to spend the holiday with us. After he arrived, he and my daughters exchanged gifts, and we laughed and talked until everyone began to get sleepy. Then my oldest daughter went home, and the rest of us went to bed.

Christmas morning was very quiet and still; my brother slept pretty late and Trenise did not want to get up at all. I could hear her in the room crying, so I went and gave her a hug and told her that it would be okay. I tried to be strong for her, but both of us just began to cry, for we were truly missing Tavi and C.J.

After my brother left to go back to Philly, Trenise and I decided to visit the location where Tavi and C.J. were killed. When we arrived, we noticed there were so many stuffed animals from various people in the neighborhood. Although they did not know Tavi and C.J., I was so grateful to them for thinking of my kids. I felt we were not carrying this grief alone.

After leaving the accident scene, we visited the gravesite, and then we went by my in-laws house to check on them because we knew they missed Tavi and C.J. as well, however we did not stay too long.

Trenise and I left to go back home, feeling hurt, sad, and alone, and that evening was very quiet. Trenise stayed in her room and I stayed in mine. I tried to get some sleep, but I just cried and kept talking to the Lord, asking Him to help me. I knew only God could and that He would!

During the month of December 2004, there was an organization that was making plans for a Martin Luther King, Jr. birthday celebration that was going to be held during the month of January. I was asked to share my testimony with other mothers who had lost a child due to gun violence on the streets of Washington, DC. My focus and attention was on what the Lord would have me to say to these moms; all the while wondering how He would have me to encourage them through their hurt and pain.

When Easter came, it was a little hard watching other parents with their children, but I was grateful that I no longer felt like I was going to have a heart attack. I knew for Easter, Mother's Day, and all the other holidays that I would not receive those homemade cards that Tavi and C.J. would bring home from school, but I did keep the very last ones from the holidays before their death.

Memorial Day and the 4th of July was a little sad, only because I would take Tavi and C.J. to the zoo and downtown, or to see the fireworks on the National Mall. God allowed me to get through without breaking down though. I could just feel the Lord carrying me and I just kept giving Him praise for allowing me to experience what the Scriptures says in Matthew 5:4 about "Blessed are they that mourn, for they shall be comforted."

No one can comfort you like Christ Jesus, for He will be all that you need Him to be!!!!!!!!

Towhanna Boston

Chapter 10

Moving Forward

During the first six months of 2005, there were a lot of things going on at work and church; plus the case was about to begin against the person being charged with Tavi and C.J.'s death.

At the same time, my daily responsibilities as a mom had changed drastically. My first grocery bill after Tavi and C.J.'s death dropped from $150.00 a week to $60.00 a week because I no longer had to purchase items such as pop tarts, chocolate ego waffles, gallons of milk, Capri Sun juices, and chocolate cupcakes. Can you imagine?

I almost had to run out of the grocery store because it was just that hard. I also no longer had to come home from work and head straight into the kitchen to prepare dinner. I actually stopped cooking, but instead would just eat a bowl of cereal and go straight to bed simply because I had no homework to check, no science projects to work on, and no showers to prepare.

Yes, I still had another child at home who would not graduate from high school until 2006, but I could not carry her grief and mine all at the same time.

Did this make me a bad mom? I don't know. I just knew that it was going to take some time to adjust to not having Tavi and C.J. around.

In the quietness, more tears began to fall. I just wanted to hear their little voices call mom 100 times, asking for snacks ………….. What a huge difference.

I could not see how I was going to get through the next hour at home, let alone the next few weeks, months, or even years! I had some choices to make; either stay stuck and drown in depression, or cry out to the Lord for help.

Guess what? I chose to cry out to the Lord with a loud voice for all the help He had for me and anyone else who chooses to cast their cares on Him.

The Lord led me to read the book of Job in The Bible where his friends said he must have sinned for all these trials to be upon him. Well I have found that things don't always happen because you have sinned. God is God; He does what He wants, when He wants, and how He wants.

In the book of Job, satan had to receive permission from God in order to do what he did in Job's life. Job had seven sons and three daughters and lost all ten of his children in the same day. Losing both of my little ones was hard, but can you imagine Job's pain of losing all ten of his children?

Guess what Job did - he still bowed down and worshipped God!

Hold To God's Unchanging Hands

You might ask yourself, how in the world can somebody think about giving God praise in the same second, minute, or hour of finding out that your child or children have died? Well, it is not easy or possible if you do not know the Lord or have a relationship with Him.

Job feared God and walked up right before Him, so you can say that he knew the Lord as his Savior. Instead of being angry with God, and instead of blaming God, he made a choice to give God praise.

PRAISE BREAK.......take a minute and think about your loss, trial, situation, or test that you may even be in right now and how the enemy has desired to use it to destroy you......and how the Lord is keeping you even in the midst of it....whew; I have to praise God!!!!!   ~shouting~

We have to remember that we are created for God's purpose and for His Glory! I do believe that our trials are designed to work things out of us so the Lord can deposit more of His characteristics into us. Sometimes He is trying to get our attention as well as those around us. Some have not realized that yet, but we must be available for God's plan and purpose for our lives.

Many people have been known to grieve from three to ten years with their hearts hurting, and tears flowing while they sink deep into depression. Grabbing hold to God's unchanging hands will help you get through this process. I am not saying the process will be shorter, but when you hold onto God's hands, it can be gentler than if you are trying to go through it without His help.

Know that you do not have to stay stuck because that's exactly what the enemy wants you to do. The Lord will help and condition you in the midst of every loss, trial, heartache, test, or situation. We shall live and not die because it is only a test that we must pass!!!!

I am not saying that you should not be angry because the Scripture says in Ephesians 4:26 that we can be angry but sin not! And yes, you can ask God why, but it is the attitude in which you ask or approach Him.

In the midst of your loss, pain, tears, trials, or test, it is alright to ask God "why" and for clarity because we need directions, and we need to know what to do next or even where we need to go from here! We must keep in mind that our loss, pain, tears, trials, or tests are not only about us, but it's about God's will being done in our lives so that His purpose is fulfilled and so that He may get all the Glory!

I truly believe the Lord knows what is best for our lives and for Tavi and C.J. The Lord could see their future; He could see down the road where as I could not, therefore He chose to call them home to be with Him.

Tavi and C.J. were happy children, so I did not want to walk around sad, angry, or depressed. I knew and believed that only God could heal me and He had to teach me to embrace Him during my moments of missing them. The Lord let me know that it is okay to cry because as their mother I will always miss them until we meet again in Glory!

Since the time of Tavi and C.J.'s passing, I have been blessed to share with others how I am able to still stand and function, which is only because of God and the prayers of so many saints. Just know that He will carry you too!

Chapter 11

Accountability

During the first six to eight months after Tavi and C.J.'s death, I had to continue to pray, praise, and press for God to help me with my attitude towards everyone that I felt was responsible. I was not present at the time they were killed, therefore most of the information I received about the circumstances surrounding their death was based on investigative reports.

Various reports indicated the accident was caused by a criminal who was fleeing police during a high speed chase in a residential neighborhood in Washington, DC.

My children were struck and killed by the suspect as they were walking in a crosswalk. I was told that the impact was so intense, that it knocked them out of their shoes, sending them 140 feet into the air, which caused them to die instantly when their little bodies hit the ground.

Now from what I was also told, they were at a traffic light, which changed, signaling for them to cross the street. Their father initially had their hands, but as they proceeded to cross, they let go of his hand and grabbed each other's hand. It was at this point that they entered into the crosswalk and were struck by the fleeing suspect, who was driving at a very high rate of speed.

The District of Columbia Police Department has a "No Chase Law" where the police are not supposed to conduct a chase in residential areas unless the suspect is armed or presents a danger, and in this case, the suspect was not armed. The police did not accept responsibility for Tavi and C.J.'s death because they stated they had ended the chase several blocks prior to where the accident occurred, however the fleeing suspect continued driving at a very high rate of speed.

Based on what I saw from the news coverage which included eyewitness accounts, it was questionable as to whether or not the police were still chasing the suspect, however the police department felt as though they did nothing wrong, and therefore refused to accept responsibility or issue an apology for what took place.   In fact, the suspect also did not apologize until his sentencing.

I continued to ask myself over and over and over again, whether or not the police actually had any responsibility in causing Tavi and C.J.'s death, and if so, I felt that they should have been held responsible for their role as well as issued an apology.

Now as far as the children's dad was concerned, I often wondered if things would have turned out differently had he been holding their hands.   I don't know, but these are questions that I often wondered about.

Because I was not there when the accident happened, I felt like I only had bits and pieces of the story.   I often feel like had I been there, I would have been holding their hands, however I truly believe that no matter who had their hands, if the Lord wanted Tavi and C.J. to come home to be with Him, then that's exactly what was supposed to happen. When it is each of our time, nobody will be able to stop it from happening because we all have our set time that the Lord will call us home.

I was however very grateful for the people in the neighborhood because they pitched in to help catch the suspect after he bailed out of his car and tried to flee on foot. We are taught to take responsibility for our actions and life is full of choices, which some of the choices that people make are not so wise.

I had to pray hard for the Lord to help me to forgive the police as well as the suspect. There was a time when every time I saw a police officer, I was consumed with hate because of what happened to my children, because of the fact that the suspect was initially fleeing from the police. While I was experiencing a great deal of pain as it relates to who I felt was responsible for causing my children's death, I also realized that the way I was feeling was totally taking me out of character.

I do however pray that each police officer who was on duty that day and those who were involved in the case would give their life to the Lord because we definitely need some saved, Holy Ghost filled police officers working our streets.

Since that time, the Lord has truly worked on me and given me so much peace, which only came after much prayer, praise, and press. I remained determined to keep my mind on Jesus as complete healing took place.

Lord I just want to thank you, Lord I just want to thank you!!!!

Towhanna Boston

Chapter 12

The Final Decision

This chapter leads up to the sentencing of the person charged with the deaths of Octavia Michelle Suydan and Christopher Edward Suydan Jr., my precious angels.

The first meeting was called a Status Hearing, which is when the prosecutor and defense attorney would discuss where they were in the case as far as gathering evidence, as well as other charges that could potentially be brought against the suspect. This was also the first time I had come face-to-face with the person who was being charged with Tavi and C.J.'s death. My brother-in-law attended the hearing with me so that I would not be alone.

The Status Hearing was pretty short. I clearly remember the suspect's face, looking as if everything was great. He was also very happy to see his girlfriend who showed up to support him.

As we sat there listening to the judge ask both attorneys questions, I was thinking, how can this young man be in such a good mood when he is being charged for killing two precious children.

During the Status Hearing, the suspect accepted a plea bargain, which meant there was a chance that the case would not go to trial.

Apparently someone advised him that by pleading guilty, he would get less time, meaning a much shorter sentence.

I could not believe it!

Perhaps the city also felt the plea bargain would save them a lot of money too, however if the case did not go to trial, it would not allow us to learn the full details of what really happened the day Tavi and C.J. were killed.

After both attorneys finished exchanging information with the judge, a date was set for the next hearing, which was called an Agreement Hearing. This type of hearing was so the prosecuting attorney and the defense attorney, along with the parents of the deceased, could come to an agreement on whether the case should go to trial, or go straight to sentencing because of the plea bargain.

During the time in between the Status Hearing and the Agreement Hearing, I continued to pray and ask the Lord for guidance as I journeyed through what I anticipated would result in unimaginable disappointment and pain.

The children's father asked me, "Why do you want a trial?"

I said, "Because I was not there and a trial would clear up the bits and pieces that I felt were missing from what I received in various reports."

Then he went on to explain that a trial would drag the process out, meaning time missed from work, and not to mention all the hurtful details surrounding the kids' death, which may cause me to suffer an additional setback of hurt and pain.

I told him, "I don't think so, because as long as I have JESUS, I will be alright!"

During the Agreement Hearing, the suspect entered a guilty plea, then the judge set the sentencing date. At the request of the defense team, a six week extension was granted.

I did not understand why they needed an extension when the suspect had already pleaded guilty.

While we were waiting for the new sentencing date, I received a letter from the courts requesting feedback on how Tavi and C.J.'s death had affected my life. I was also given information on who to contact when it came time for the suspect to be paroled, and I was also advised that we would be allowed to speak and express ourselves during the Sentencing.

I filled out all the papers, answering each question, which included questions like: Was the law fulfilled in this case? How have our lives changed? Would we like to give words before the judge handed down the sentence?

I mailed everything back to the judge, along with a copy of the program from Tavi and C.J.'s home going service because I wanted the judge to see the type of kids Tavi and C.J. were. I also shared in my response that I disagreed with the plea bargain and requested for the judge to give the suspect the maximum sentence available in this case.

Once I was done, I continued to pray for the judge and the attorneys, as well as the suspect who was being charged for the death of my children.

It was so very important for me to stay prayerful because during the time that we would be allowed to speak, I did not want to explode and go off on everyone involved in this case. Instead, I wanted them to see Christ in me, so I needed the Lord to help me speak in a manner that would be pleasing to Him.

The Lord let me know that everything was going to be OK and He allowed a calmness to come over me. I knew everything was in God's hands, and no matter what the sentence would be, God was still in control. I thank the Lord for allowing me to forgive the suspect and I prayed that at some point he would receive salvation.

Only God can take something bad and turn it into good!!!!!

Now it was bad that Tavi and C.J.'s lives were taken at such an early age, but the good that came out of all this is the four souls that went down in water baptism in Jesus Name after Bishop Johnson preached "Will You Be Ready". During the sermon, Bishop Johnson spoke of Noah and how once the ark was finished and the rain began, so many were not ready!

God is and will continue to get all the glory in this entire situation!

Now the day had come for the sentencing hearing. I went to work for most of the morning, and my daughter Trenise went with me because we had to be at the courthouse at 12:45 PM.

When we arrived at the courthouse, I remember some reporters being present and some of the suspect's family members, as well as Chris.

It started a little late because we were waiting for the judge to arrive. I was the first person to speak and I let the judge and everyone under the sound of my voice know that God and only God had allowed me to forgive the suspect, even though he had not yet apologized for killing Tavi and C.J. I also stated that I hoped he would use the time the judge gave him to serve to think about what he had done and also repent and surrender his life to the Lord!

Once I was finished speaking, it was Chris' turn to speak. When he got up to speak, the authorities formed a circle around the suspect because they thought Chris was going to jump over the rails and attack him. Chris was so angry and was yelling extremely loud to the point that I thought he was going to be thrown out of there, but the judge let him vent as loud and for as long as he wanted.

He expressed how hard Father's Day would be and how the day of the sentencing hearing was my birthday and the kids were not here to say Happy Birthday to me. I just sat there and cried quietly. My daughter was being comforted by two of my friends, who accompanied us for emotional support.

Once Chris finished speaking, the prosecuting attorney gave his statement explaining what took place on that tragic day and the choices the suspect could have made instead of running that red light, which led to the death of two precious children.

When it was time for the defense attorney to speak, he stated that we all have done foolish things at the age of 19, which is not true for all people especially in terms of causing someone else to lose their life.

In my opinion, the suspect's age had nothing to do with the choice he made to flee the police and run that red light, which led to my little angels' lives being taken. What we also learned was the suspect had just recently been in trouble with the law, where he was told not to return back to the neighborhood where my children were struck and killed. As a result, he was already on probation.

As I listened to the judge state how she viewed each fact surrounding the details of the case and because of the way she spoke to the suspect, I was certain she would give him at least 20 to 25 years. When the sentence was handed down and the judge said 16 years and 8 months, I was shocked! I could not believe he only received 16 years and 8 months for killing both Tavi and C.J.!

Chris stormed out of the court room. Then my daughter Trenise went storming out next. I just sat there in complete shock with this blank look on my face.

I could not believe what I had just heard......wow, are you kidding me – 16 years for taking two lives!!!!!

At that moment, I knew I needed the Lord then as never before! ~tears~

I was in such a daze! After that, I could not find my daughter. As I finally proceeded outside the courthouse, there were so many reporters asking if I had a moment to express my thoughts regarding the judge's decision.

I remember one reporter asking me why I forgave the suspect.

I responded, "Because God has forgiven me and others from the wrong we have done. If we expect God to forgive us, we must forgive others."

Hold To God's Unchanging Hands

As I stated before, God is in complete control!!!

I also shared with the reporters that the laws are too lenient on these young people who are out here breaking the laws.

The prison system is like a revolving door for a lot of our youth, and if the young man charged in Tavi and C.J.'s death does not turn his life around, he will most likely end up right back in jail shortly after he is released.

Even though I know God has kept me and is continuing to keep me, the judge's sentence was another hard pill to swallow!!!

After I was not able to find my daughter, I ended up walking back to my job hoping to find her there. When I arrived at my office, I saw my daughter with her head down crying, so I told her, "Let's go home."

Once we got home, I called my oldest daughter Kesha to share the details about the sentencing and the questions from the reporters. After that, I just needed to rest because by this time I was emotionally and physically drained. I expressed praise to the Lord for getting me through, and went to sleep.

Know that prayer, praise and pressing has sustained me and will sustain you too!!!!!! Hold to God's unchanging Hands.

Towhanna Boston

Chapter 13

Knowing Your Purpose In Christ

Many people often sit in church for years, but do not know what they are supposed to be doing for the Lord in building the Kingdom. Take a few moments and ask yourself these questions: Am I walking in my Purpose? Really?

Do you really know what you are supposed to be doing for Jesus?

I remember asking the Lord what it was that He had designed for me to do for the up building of His Kingdom. While waiting on the Lord for clarity, I continued to remind myself of His Word in Proverbs 18:16 that says "Your gift will make room for you and bring you before great men."

At that time, I was singing on the choir and I had been working in the prison ministry for 10 years, but I was determined not to be busy doing all of that and not fulfilling my true purpose in Christ.

The calamity of losing Tavi and C.J. was a huge adjustment that guided me not just towards singing in the choir, which was within my comfort zone, but it also helped to move me into my purpose in Christ. At first, I was still not one hundred percent sure what the Lord was doing, so I remained prayerful in seeking clarity on what to do in coping with the loss of my babies and the fact that they were never coming back.

During this time, I still had many sad moments and tears, but the Lord continued to present situations for me to assist others who had experienced the loss of loved ones. I would get phone calls from saints, friends, co-workers, and family members asking if I would talk to someone they knew and share my testimony of God's grace while dealing with the death of my kids. At first I was hesitant because it wasn't just those who suffered the loss of a child, but it was people who had experienced various types of losses.

This went on for about two years, and then I said yes Lord, whatever Your will is for me, that is what I want to do. At that point, I enrolled in the Counseling Psychology Graduate program in the Fall of 2006, which was exactly two years after Tavi and C.J.'s death.

Obtaining a counseling degree was necessary in order for me to have the credentials needed to assist and counsel the unsaved as well as the saved. This is particularly the case when dealing with grief counseling because there may have been various issues with loved ones that could lead to complicated grief if the relationship with the person lost was complicated, or if there was a strong attachment to the person.

My goal was to be able to assist those traveling down this unbearable path of grief as they learned to cope with not having the person around anymore and accepting the adjustment that must now take place. We must get to the place where we realize that nobody can heal us but Jesus, but having someone to talk to who has experienced similar or the same type of ordeal that you are now experiencing helps a great deal.

The Lord also allowed me to start reaching out in the community by becoming a bereavement volunteer with Hospice of the Chesapeake in Landover, MD. I started working with the grief counselor there by assisting with follow-up calls to families that had just recently lost a loved one, which I still continue to do to this day. This also allowed me to realize what the Lord was calling me to do; so I still had to continue to pray for strength and guidance from the Lord, while keeping in mind that calamities are events in our lives that bring terrible loss, lasting challenges, and total distress in the midst of these tragedies. It is in the midst of the journey through our pain, loss, trials, and situations that we must know that Jesus is the help we need to arise from life's challenges in order to move into our purpose.

One example of being there to assist someone else through their loss was when a friend of mine called and asked me to speak with a friend of her daughter who recently lost her mother, whom she was extremely close to. This girl was not doing well at all due to not having her mother anymore and she began traveling down a path of self-destruction. I said I would come to see her that following Sunday after church. For the rest of the week I remained in prayer for this girl and asked the Lord to speak through me and touch her heart so that she would receive what God wanted her to hear. I went to meet with her on that Sunday and we instantly clicked. She was very comfortable opening up to me and I gave God all the Glory.

When someone is dealing with deep, complicated grief, it is not always easy for them to open up to someone else.

My visit with the young lady went well and then when I saw her a year later, she was doing a lot better. She had begun to focus on investing that negative energy into something positive in keeping her mother's memory alive. God is great and greatly to be praised in all things!!!

The impact of Tavi and C.J.'s death has caused my faith to be strengthened in Christ and has allowed me to remain focused on the will of God for my life.

Do I miss Tavi and C.J.? Yes indeed, very much and I will always miss them, however now I am able to attend events that have families there with their children without crying or feeling down. I am able to spend time with my grandson and god children without falling apart or isolating myself from the rest of the world afterwards.

I give all the glory to God for using me as He sees fit! I continue to reach out to those who the Lord places in my path to minister to and share my testimony with, hoping it encourages them to allow God to give them complete healing and for each person to know that He has a greater plan for their lives.

Sometimes we can be so busy being involved with so many different ministries that we are not truly waiting to hear from God on what our true purpose is in Him!! Some ministries we have called ourselves to just to gain status and titles, but I want to encourage you today not to waste any more valuable time. Stop, think, and seek God in order to know your true purpose in Christ. DO NOT leave this world not having done what God has called or purposed in you to do!

St. Matthew 6:33 tells us "But seek ye first the kingdom of God, and His righteousness; and all these things shall be added unto you."

Know that your test, trials, and loss are not just about you going through, but it is also about the things that God has and is truly calling you to do for His Kingdom. Ask God for clarity, direction, and help in what you are to do. Do not worry about people thinking you are crazy, or even talking bad about you, but all that matters is that you are doing the will of God.

They lied on Jesus, so they will lie on you; they talked bad about Jesus, so they will talk bad about you; they persecuted Jesus, so they will persecute you, but at the end of the day what matters is your obedience to the will of God!!!

As you journey through life's trials, know with assurance that God has your back, and He will carry you, He will guide you, and He will keep you if you trust and obey Him.

Do what the Lord is calling you to do, and know that it is not about titles, status, or popularity, but IT'S ALLLLLLLLLLLL ABOUT JESUS!!!!!

Walk in purpose so that Jesus gets all the Glory out of your life according to St. John 9:4, which states "I must work the works of Him that sent me, while it is day ....the night cometh when no man can work."

DO NOT LET IT BE SAID TOO LATE!

Towhanna Boston

Chapter 14

Hold to God's Unchanging Hands

My mind goes back to this song entitled – "Without Him" where the lyrics go:

Without Him, I could do nothing
Without Him, I'd surely fail
Without Him, I would be drifting
Like a ship without a sail

Jesus is the source of our very being; He is the reason for our very existence today and everyday!

Acts 17:28 also tells us, "For in Him we live, and move, and have our being."

I am only standing because of Jesus
I am only standing because of God's Grace
I am only standing because of God's Mercy
I am only standing because of JESUS and He does all things well!

If you or someone in your life has been affected by a tragedy that has been caused by another person, I want to encourage you today to ask God to help you to forgive that person or persons.

Forgiveness is so important in your healing process, especially as you attempt to move forward with your life while not having your loved one that is gone because of the actions of someone else. The longer you hold on to the anger, the harder it makes the journey through that loss, trial, hurt, pain, and situation. Not forgiving that person will not bring your loved one back and as hard as it is, you must ask the Lord to help you to accept what God has allowed.

This loss, hurt, pain and challenge is about you now moving to where God is trying to take you in Him because in this life there are stages and levels that you must reach as you accept your purpose.

If it were not for our losses, pain, hurt, and challenges, many people would never move forward into their purpose because of wanting to stay in their comfort zone.

For most of us, God has to push us towards our next level in Him and He did not create us so we can stay at the same place in our lives. He has a plan for each of us and I want to encourage you to allow the Lord to use that test that you currently are in, that loss that you have just suffered, that challenge that seems to be unbearable, and let the Lord use it for His Glory. Pray and seek His will for your life while you are in the heat of that loss, that pain, or that test!!!!

Stay focused on what the Lord is asking you to do; praise Him as He guides you in your purpose, and then press your way, allowing God to use you to help others. Jesus will use your hurt for a greater work for the Glory of God!!!! Hallelujah……..

Holding to God's unchanging hands was the best decision I could have ever made after losing Tavi and C.J.

Hold To God's Unchanging Hands

Be encouraged and know that because Jesus is the same, yesterday, today and forever, He will never leave us and He is here to carry us through every loss, trial, test, situation, pain, and every difficult time in our lives.

Continue to pray your way through, praise your way through, and press your way toward your purpose in Christ Jesus so that He gets the Glory out of your life, in Jesus Name, AMEN!

Towhanna Boston

About the Author

Towhanna A. Boston was born and raised in the city of Brotherly Love, Philadelphia, PA. Her early education was also completed in her hometown. As a full-time mother of four wonderful children, Towhanna successfully completed her Bachelor of Science Degree in Business Administration from Strayer University in Washington, DC. She is currently pursuing her Master of Arts Degree in Counseling Psychology at Bowie State University in Bowie, MD.

On September 11, 2004 Towhanna tragically lost her two youngest children, C.J., age 7, and Tavi, age 8, during an accident that resulted from a suspect who was fleeing from police at a high rate of speed in the District of Columbia. Towhanna has found strength in her sorrow that has flourished into an encouraging voice to those who have suffered the excruciating pain of losing a loved one.

Towhanna volunteers for Hospice of the Chesapeake, serving as a bereavement volunteer, as well as participating in community outreach events. Towhanna has also been invited to speak at various events throughout the DC Metropolitan Area.

To contact Towhanna to share her testimony or to assist someone in coping with the loss of a loved one, forward requests by e-mail to holdtoGod624@yahoo.com or call 240.389.7343.

If you would like to provide feedback, please visit www.taviandcjlives.weebly.com .

Towhanna Boston

About Kingdom Journey Press

Kingdom Journey Press, Inc. is a full-service publishing company specializing in providing customized services to support our clients from the conception of an idea to getting HIStory to the masses! Since the time of inception and in conjunction with our umbrella organization, Kingdom Journey Enterprises, we have become recognized globally for our ability to establish a unique presence, while building relationships with partners and clients consisting of current and aspiring writers, and ministry, business, and community organizations.

Our services include:

- ❖ Manuscript Evaluation
- ❖ Coaching for current and aspiring authors
- ❖ Editing
- ❖ Cover and Print Layout Design
- ❖ Print and E-Book Format
- ❖ Copyright and Distribution
- ❖ Marketing and Sales Support

To contact us and to learn more information about our services, we invite you to visit our website at www.kjpressinc.com.

Towhanna Boston